WOULD YOU RATHER?

Our team has put a lot of work into creating this book, we would be grateful for sharing your opinion about it.

SCAN FOR MORE PRODUCTS

be forced to sing along
or
dance to every single song you hear?

WOULD YOU RATHER...

find the love of your life
or
win $ 20 million in the lottery?

that your friends know
all your secrets
             or
that all people in the world
know your thoughts?

WOULD YOU RATHER...

lose all your senses
          or
forget about memories

have free internet for life
or
free coffee for life?

WOULD YOU RATHER...

to walk in a nice but biting
sweater for a week
or
an ugly but comfy sweater?

to live forever without electronic
or
to life without washing?

WOULD YOU RATHER...

*labor under a hot sun
or
extreme cold?*

never be able to go out during
the day
or
never be able to go out at night?

WOULD YOU RATHER...

to have a nice but stupid
partner
or
an ugly but smart partner?

never be able to write
a text message
or
never be able to call

WOULD YOU RATHER...

live all year round in high heat
or
live all year in frost

to smell dirty socks
or
to smell the poop?

WOULD YOU RATHER...

to have an annoying mother, a
great mother-in-law
or
an annoying mother-in-law,
and a great mother?

to have twenty cats and one dog
or
twenty dogs and one cat?

WOULD YOU RATHER...

to sing well, but to dance
hopelessly
or
to sing hopelessly and dance
well?

listen to Christmas carols
all the time
or
to a musical genre you don't like?

WOULD YOU RATHER...

be an hour late
or
two hours earlier?

live in a haunted hour
or
live with your enemies?

WOULD YOU RATHER...

to have rats at home
or
to have snakes at home?

be able to turn back time
or
fast forward time?

WOULD YOU RATHER...

turn into a cat for one day
or
turn into a tiger?

have a constant feeling
of déjà vu
or
feel drunk?

WOULD YOU RATHER...

never be able to eat chocolate
or
be forced to eat chocolate
with every meal?

get a paper cut every time
you turn page
or
bite your tongue every
time you eat?

WOULD YOU RATHER...

be constantly thirsty
or
be hungry?

be a two-year-old

or

20 years older?

WOULD YOU RATHER...

to star in an Oscar-winning
film

or

get Grammy for the song?

be a two-year-old
or
20 years older?

WOULD YOU RATHER...

to star in an Oscar-winning
film
or
get Grammy for the song?

die before
or
after your partner?

WOULD YOU RATHER...

have eight children year after
year
or
have four children every 5
years?

fart on a first date
or
fart on our wedding night?

WOULD YOU RATHER...

know everything
or
be able to do everything?

have a big pimple
on your forehead
or
smell like fish?

WOULD YOU RATHER...

to have a beer factory
or
to have your own vineyard?

have a poorly paid job but one
you like
or
a well paid job you don't like?

WOULD YOU RATHER...

have a lot of moles on the
body or
have a lot of freckles on the
body?

have to wear every shirt inside
out
or
every pair of pants backwards?

WOULD YOU RATHER...

wear too big clothes
or
wear too big shoes?

to be known for something
stupid
or
to be completely forgotten?

WOULD YOU RATHER...

lose the ability to read
or
lose the ability to speak?

start a new life among
strangers in a big city
or
start a new life in the
countryside with your loved
ones?

WOULD YOU RATHER...

sleep in a doghouse
or
let stray dogs sleep in your
bed?

live for a week in a lot of noise
or
live for a week in total silence?

WOULD YOU RATHER...

for everyone to read your
texts
or
see all the pictures on your
phone?

to have irrepressible laughter
at the funeral of a loved one
or
a crying attack at your own
wedding?

WOULD YOU RATHER...

be smart but boring
or
be stupid but go-getting?

people knew all the details of
your finances
or
all the details of your love life?

WOULD YOU RATHER...

clean up a loved one's vomit
or
clean up a loved one's shit

not to have one eye
or
not to have one ear?

WOULD YOU RATHER...

get your paycheck given to
you in pennies
or
never be able to use cash
again?

look young at 80 but be insane
or
look old at 30 but be
mentally fit?

WOULD YOU RATHER...

to live 70 years unhappy
or
live 20 years happily?

to be overheard
or
watched?

WOULD YOU RATHER...

*have fortune
or
fame?*

have police hunting you down
for a crime you didn't commit
or
a serial killer actually hunting
you?

WOULD YOU RATHER...

steal Duchess Meghan
or
Duchess Kate's style?

will you never feel pain again
or
will you never feel pleasure
again?

WOULD YOU RATHER...

still have chills
or
still have hiccups?

to cheat on a partner
or
to be cheated?

WOULD YOU RATHER...

eat burnt dishes
or
eat raw foods?

forget something constantly
or
lie maniacally?

WOULD YOU RATHER...

be stranded in the jungle
or
in the desert?

never watch a movie again
or
never read a book again?

WOULD YOU RATHER...

spend every weekend indoors
or
spend every weekend
outdoors?

party for free all year round
or
travel for free all year round?

WOULD YOU RATHER...

discover a new planet
or
discover a new chemical
element?

marry the most attractive
person you've ever met
or
the best cook you've ever
met?

WOULD YOU RATHER...

change sex for one day
or
become a ghost for one day?

wear real fur
or
fake jewels?

WOULD YOU RATHER...

never drink coffee
or
never eat sweets?

wear only pink clothes for a
month
or
wear only white clothes for a
month?

WOULD YOU RATHER...

get drunk off of one sip of
alcohol
or
never get drunk no matter
how much booze you imbibe?

eat a fried mouse
or
a cooked spider?

WOULD YOU RATHER...

be a criticized
or
be ignored?

to be a master in cooking
or
be a master in kissing?

WOULD YOU RATHER...

never age physically
or
never age mentally?

have a headache all week
or
feel a burning sensation
throughout the week?

WOULD YOU RATHER...

lose all of your teeth
or
all of your hair?

look cute but have a gross
voice
or
look ugly but have a sweet
voice?

WOULD YOU RATHER...

to have rich but false friends
or
to have poor but loyal
friends?

resurrect Michael Jackson
or
Elvis Presley?

WOULD YOU RATHER...

have excessive body hair
or
acne all over your body?

be a genius everyone thinks is
an idiot
or
an idiot everyone thinks is a
genius?

WOULD YOU RATHER...

*be color blind
or
lose your sense of taste?*

be a genius everyone thinks is an idiot
or
an idiot everyone thinks is a genius?

WOULD YOU RATHER...

have tea with Queen Elizabeth
or
a beer with Prince William?

smell other people's feet after
a whole day
or
lick someone's hands after
visiting the toilet

WOULD YOU RATHER...

eat soup with tangle of hair
or
eat a steak with bits of nails?

always having to say what
you think
or
never being able to say
anything again?

WOULD YOU RATHER...

to kiss a frog
or
a crocodile?

to have your grandfather's
hairstyle
or
your grandmother's teeth?

WOULD YOU RATHER...

live on the streets for a week
or
sleep in bed with the ex you
hate the most for one night?

have lice
or
have a tapeworm?

WOULD YOU RATHER...

be stuck with someone who
talked non-stop
or
be stuck on an island all
alone?

be attacked by a pack of bears
or
a pack of wolves?

WOULD YOU RATHER...

nine toes
or
an extra nipple?

having to sit all day
or
stand all day?

WOULD YOU RATHER...

walk lying down
or
sleep standing up?

Printed in Great Britain
by Amazon

50708643R00032